Eleanor Roosevelt

A Friend to All

THE UNIVERSAL DECLARATION
OF Human Rights

Tamara Hollingsworth

Consultant

Glenn Manns, M.A.
Teaching American History Coordinator
Ohio Valley Educational Cooperative

Publishing Credits

Dona Herweck Rice, *Editor-in-Chief*; Lee Aucoin, *Creative Director*; Conni Medina, M.A.Ed., *Editorial Director*; Jamey Acosta, *Associate Editor*; Neri Garcia, *Senior Designer*; Stephanie Reid, *Photo Researcher*; Rachelle Cracchiolo, M.A.Ed., *Publisher*

Image Credits

Teacher Created Materials

5301 Oceanus Drive
Huntington Beach, CA 92649-1030
http://www.tcmpub.com

ISBN 978-1-4333-1591-6

© 2011 Teacher Created Materials, Inc.
Made in China
Nordica.052015.CA21500197

Table of Contents

Hello, Eleanor

Eleanor Roosevelt (ROH-zuh-velt) was a woman of action. When she saw a problem, she tried to fix it. Her life was not always easy. But she worked to make life better for others. Today, people remember her as a kind and fair woman.

Eleanor helping children

Fun Fact

Eleanor was once called "a friend to all mankind."

Eleanor enjoyed knitting when she traveled.

Young Eleanor

Young Eleanor

Eleanor was born in New York on October 11, 1884. When she was young, her mother and her father died. Eleanor's grandmother sent her away to school in England. She was a good student. But she worried that she was not good enough.

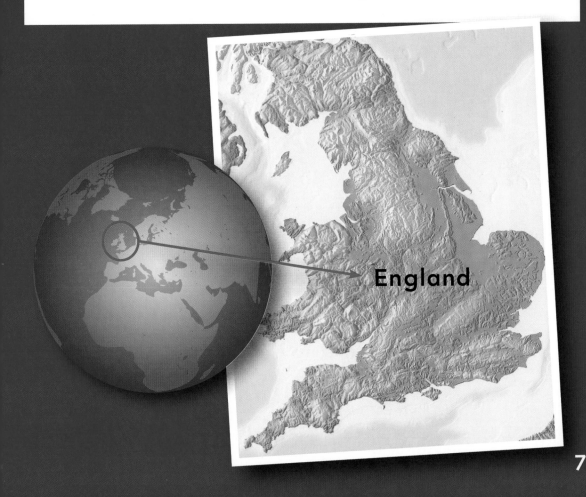

England

When Eleanor was 17, she met Franklin Roosevelt on a train trip. He liked the strong, smart Eleanor. They fell in love. Finally, they got married on March 17, 1905. They had six children.

Eleanor and Franklin at their wedding

Eleanor

Eleanor with Franklin and their family

Franklin with Fala, the family
dog, and a friend's little girl

Life Changes

In 1921, Franklin got very ill. After the sickness, he could not move his legs. He began using a wheelchair. Eleanor would not let Franklin give up. She told him not to let the wheelchair change his plans.

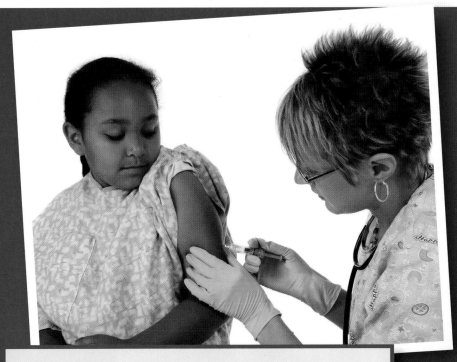

Franklin was sick with **polio** (POH-lee-oh). Today, we have a special shot that protects us from polio.

In 1933, Franklin was elected **president** of the United States. Eleanor became **First Lady**. Times were hard in America. Many people did not have jobs. Eleanor wanted to help. She traveled around the country asking people what they needed.

People stood in long lines for free bread.

Today this hard time is known as the Great Depression.

Eleanor and Franklin

Franklin becomes president

Eleanor making a speech

Eleanor, the First Lady

Eleanor helped Franklin with his work as president. She also did her own work. Eleanor said women should be treated the same as men. She wrote articles and gave speeches about her ideas. Her work helped change the lives of women.

This woman sews at a factory.

Fun Fact

Eleanor helped pass laws to keep women from working all day without breaks.

Back then, many people thought **African Americans** and white people should stay apart. Eleanor said skin color did not matter. She was in a club that would not let a famous African American singer sing in their hall. That singer was Marian Anderson. Eleanor got mad. She quit the club.

Marian and Eleanor

Eleanor helped Marian put on a bigger show at the Lincoln Memorial instead.

Eleanor with her dog Fala

Eleanor wanted Americans to think of her as a friend. She started writing for a newspaper. She told stories about being the president's wife. She shared her ideas. People liked getting to know her.

MY DAY
By Mrs. Eleanor Roosevelt

EASTPORT, Maine, Sunday—We are having the most wonderful weather, but even for this cool spot, it is warm and almost breathless. Yesterday morning, on the water, it was cool and we had a grand breeze on our way over to Eastport. Once landed there, we took a taxi and went out to Quoddy Village to visit the NYA resident project.

I had not seen this project since it had been turned over to the boys. I was impressed by the excellence of the work shops and by the tremendous interest which the boys show in the work they are doing in aviation mechanics and the regular machine shops. They have good classrooms and have set up an instrument room now, because they found a demand for men who could work on instruments.

The gliders they are making are extraordinarily good, and I hope the Army will send somebody up to inspect them, because I feel they could be used for experimental purposes. an airfield is being built quite nearby, so that some day they will actually see their engines take a plane off the grounds, we hope.

PERHAPS the most exciting part of this project is the actual practice of democracy. The law allows no discrimination of race or religion, and these boys have entered into the spirit of real democracy. Since they govern themselves, they see to it that no discrimination exists. They have a mayor, a council and a court. They also hold elections.

They had called a meeting a agreed that, though it was a Saturday, these boys knew that I would want to see them at work. It was decided to take Wednesday afternoon off and to work yesterday morning; no one was to ask me for autographs while I walked around.

I saw them have dinner. The food is good and yet they do it on 38 cents per boy per day. They plan a full recreational program and seem interested and happy. I think the NYA project at Quoddy is a very valuable project, for it seems to be turning out good men.

Fun Fact

Eleanor wrote her newspaper column six days a week for many years!

Eleanor was an important woman who had a lot of money. But she took time to talk to all types of people. She was a good listener. She asked factory workers and farmers how she could help them. She stuck up for women and African Americans. People said she was friendly and caring.

Eleanor reading to children

Fun Fact

Eleanor changed the job of a First Lady. She used the job to help people.

A painting of Eleanor

Eleanor spoke often at the United Nations.

Eleanor at the United Nations

The spring of 1945 was a sad time for Eleanor. Her husband, Franklin, died. But the new president found a special job for Eleanor. He asked her to join the United Nations. She was the first woman to work for this group.

The symbol of the United Nations

Fun Fact

The United Nations is a group of people from many countries who all work together.

Many people thought a woman could not work in the United Nations. Eleanor proved them wrong. She was clever and hard working. She helped make a list of human **rights**. Rights are things that make life fair for everyone.

Eleanor wins another award.

THE UNIVERSAL DE... OF Human R...

Eleanor worked hard at her job in the United Nations.

Eleanor did many things so people could have equal rights.

Goodbye, Eleanor

Eleanor was born to a rich family. She was the president's wife. She knew that other people were not as lucky. She used her good fortune to help others. She changed many lives. Eleanor died in 1962 at the age of 78. But the world will never forget her good deeds.

Eleanor Roosevelt was loved by both young and old people all over the world.

Fun Fact

President Harry Truman called Eleanor the "First Lady of the World."

Time

1884

Eleanor Roosevelt is born in New York.

1905

Eleanor and Franklin marry.

1929

The Great Depression begins.

Line

1933
Franklin is elected President.

1945
Eleanor becomes the first woman to work in the UN.

1962
Eleanor dies at the age of 78.

Glossary

African Americans—Americans whose families came from Africa

First Lady—the wife of the president of the United States

polio—an illness that can keep a person from moving his or her muscles

president—a person who is the leader of a country

rights—what the law allows people to do, or what the law should allow people to do

United Nations—a group of countries that works together to try to solve world problems

Index

Americans Today

Michelle Obama is the first African American First Lady. She is married to President Barack Obama. During her time as first lady, Michelle works with her husband. They want to make the country the best it can be. Together they continue the work Eleanor and Franklin started many years ago.